At the C

Nick Aiken is author of *Prayers for Teenagers* (SPCK, 2003) and *Family Prayers* (SPCK, 2002, which he co-authored with Archbishop Rowan Williams). He has also written a number of other books and is presently Rector of Pyrford and Wisley in Surrey.

Tim Sudworth is Diocesan Youth Adviser for Guildford, helps plan the youth programme at Greenbelt and is on spiritual oversight of 24–7 prayer.

At the Cutting Edge

Ways 2 pray & what 2 say

Nick Aiken
and
Tim Sudworth

CANTERBURY
PRESS
Norwich

© Nick Aiken and Tim Sudworth 2003

First published in 2003 by the Canterbury Press Norwich
(a publishing imprint of Hymns Ancient & Modern Limited,
a registered charity)
St Mary's Works, St Mary's Plain,
Norwich, Norfolk, NR3 3BH

www.scm-canterburypress.co.uk

British Library Cataloguing-in-Publication data

A catalogue record for this book is available
from the British Library

ISBN 1-85311-533-9

Typeset by Rowland Phototypesetting Ltd,
Bury St Edmunds, Suffolk
Printed and bound in Great Britain by
Bookmarque, Croydon, Surrey

Contents

At the Cutting Edge

Introduction

I was not the first, and I will not be the last, to fall asleep during intercessions at church. It is easily done, you pick a comfy looking book, a hymn book or even a folded notice sheet will do. Place it on the pew shelf in front to soften the hardness of the surface, place your head on it and next thing you know the service leader is announcing the next hymn.

Saying that, I was in a prayer meeting a few years back, run by a vicar who shall remain nameless, and it had gone on for rather a long time in quite a comfy room. The vicar, realizing the meeting was coming to an end started a 'round-up prayer'. The type of prayer that starts, 'Thank you Lord for bringing us all here tonight . . .' As the prayer went on the pace of it got slower and slower and he mumbled more and more. All of a sudden there was a deafening hush in the room. People started opening one eye to see what was going on. Then, in a flash, the vicar's wife jabbed him in the ribs and he snorted back to life and offered a blessing to all around.

Over the years both Nick and I have been really challenged about how to do prayer and how to encourage others to do prayer. Through the 24–7 prayer movement and the 'Labyrinth' we have seen a new excitement among people to explore prayer more intimately, more creatively and more passionately.

We could probably come up with more times when we were bored with prayer than when we have been amazed by prayer. How many of us can say we have really gone to a 'thin place', as the Celts describe it, a time or a place where the divide between heaven and earth is at its thinnest? This book will hopefully help you in your journey of prayer, from wherever you start it.

What is Prayer?

'Prayer is conversation with God', said Clement of Alexandria, who was one of the early Christian saints, and in a nutshell that is it. Conversation for most of us is not a problem. With the people we know we usually find it easy to talk, or at least we find it easy to talk when we want to or have to.

So don't make a big deal out of prayer; it is simply talking to God about the things that concern you. And there can be a broad range of things. It could be concerns about things that worry you, or about your friends and family. It could be about some of the terrible things that happen in our world or neighbourhood. Or it could be just giving thanks for the goodness of a new day, with all its opportunities and possibilities. So prayer is just talking to God. Plain and simple.

Introduction

How do you Pray?

First by realizing that it's not just about being in a special place at a special time. God is everywhere and always with us. So you can pray wherever or whenever you like: on the bus, walking to college or work, in the car, or at a quiet moment in your room at home. You do not need an appointment with God; the door into His presence is permanently open.

You do not need to be kneeling with your eyes shut; in fact it can be a lot easier if you just sit there and carry on a conversation as if you were talking to a friend. You do not have to use long words and there are no extra points for how long your conversation is. It's just about talking.

Sometimes praying with a friend can be easier, so you might want to consider inviting a friend to come and pray with you.

If you find it difficult to concentrate, you could light a candle or use a picture of Jesus or something that spiritually inspires you as a focus (see the section 'Ideas for creative prayer' for ideas on how to do this as a group). The purpose of this book is to provoke you and get you going by using prayers that other Christians have written to help you along the way.

So go for it.

TS

Prayer in the Bible

I've been struck, in rereading the prayers of the Bible, by how much breadth of emotion they cover. Here are a few examples.

'How long, O Lord, must I cry for help, but you do not listen.'

Habakkuk 1:2

'My God, my God, why have you forsaken me?
   Why are you so far from saving me,
   so far from the words of my groaning?'

Psalm 22:1

'I will extol the Lord at all times;
   his praise will always be on my lips.
My soul will boast in the Lord;
   let the afflicted hear and rejoice.'

Psalm 34:1–2

Just three examples and three totally different emotions. If we jump forward into the New Testament, we read how Jesus used the prayers in the Old Testament in his ministry. He uses one of the examples given above (Psalm 22:1) when actually dying on the Cross:

> And at the ninth hour Jesus cried out in a loud voice, 'Eloi, Eloi, lama sabachthani?' – which means, 'My God, my God, why have you forsaken me?'
>
> Mark 15:34

Again, if we continue into the Acts of the Apostles we see the Apostles using the Old Testament as a backdrop to prayer:

> When they heard this, they raised their voices together in prayer to God. 'Sovereign Lord,' they said, 'you made the heaven and the earth and the sea, and everything in them. You spoke by the Holy Spirit through the mouth of your servant, our father David:
>
> 'Why do the nations rage and the peoples plot in vain?
>
> The kings of the earth take their stand
> and the rulers gather together against the Lord
> and against his Anointed One'
>
> (Acts 4:24–7).

A wonderful breadth of emotion and use of Old Testament prayers. Look through the history of the Church and you will find lots of examples of saints doing the same thing, different churchmanships, styles, ages and genders all praying through the ages. In this book you will find quotes about prayer from the famous and the not so famous. You will also find in the next section some ideas on how to get yourself and others excited about prayer. Through it all we hope you will find a passion common to that found in the Bible when people pray.

Ideas for creative prayer

Atmosphere – A lot of people struggle to get anyone to take prayer seriously for any length of time. What I've found is that if you have the right atmosphere it can help a lot.

- *Music* – Particularly chill-out session CDs or some of Jonny Baker's work (www.proost.co.uk) are the best to use. If you go to a large music store you can often find CDs of Gregorian Chant as well.
- *Decor* – Reduced lighting always helps, maybe with some slide projectors putting images on the wall. Slides of old stained glass windows can be bought easily from cathedral bookshops or from the internet.
- *Scent* – Smells are often under-used – incense sticks, thuribles, or aromatherapy oils add quite a nice feel to any prayer room.

Here are some ideas to help you fill out a room for creative prayer.

Mosaic – Romans used mosaics to show how important or wealthy a household was. If you go to a local DIY centre you can buy blank ceramic tiles quite cheaply.

Once you've brought them, paint them all different colours, let them dry, then smash them into little bits. If you focus the prayer time on a particular verse in the Bible or a particular issue then get a group to quietly plan and make a mosaic picture. Use PVA glue to stick the broken tiles to a piece of MDF.

Picture Cross – If you are doing a prayer session over Easter this is a really good idea. Get several pieces of acetate and glue them together, to make a square with watered down PVA (half water half glue) then raid your cupboard or other people's cupboards for *unwanted* negatives, particularly of people. Cut them into single negatives and place them in a bowl. Blu-Tack the acetate to a window and draw a cross outline on it. As people come to pray for individuals they can glue a picture of them on to the window, creating a cross of faces. If you pre-plan this, people could bring negatives of particular people they want to pray for.

Wailing Wall – A simple exercise where you can paint a few boxes, then stick them together with Velcro strips to make a wall for people to stick post-it note prayers on to. To make the boxes look more like a wall add half a cup of sand to the paint and mix well.

Places – Buy an *A to Z* of the area you live in, and then cut it up in to squares. Place all the squares into a pot and suggest that people take the squares home and commit to prayer for that area for a week. This can be adapted for a world picture using an atlas and a copy of *Operation World*, or check the Operation World website on www.gmi.org, to help inform the prayers.

Icons – Set aside a wall that can be completely covered in cheap paper (available in most stationers). Cover the surrounding floor in bin liners and tape them down to save any floor area being covered with paint. Then at various different points on the wall, place, or project, icons from different cultures, churches and traditions. Supply the group with paints, pencils and felt-tip pens and get them to paint their own icons. They could also trace the outline of a projected icon on to the paper and then fill in the colours.

Symbols – Decorate a corner of a room with lots of different symbols from our culture – Nike, Adidas, McDonald's, money, etc. Among these place symbols of Christianity – a loaf of bread, a cross, wine, crown of thorns, etc.

Water – Most DIY shops now sell indoor fountains, or table-top fountains. In a room set out for prayer and reflection a fountain can add masses of atmosphere.

PART ONE

Prayers for when you want to give praise and thanks

For when you want to give praise and thanks

> I pray on the principle that wine knocks the cork out of a bottle. There is an inward fermentation, and there must be a vent. *Henry Ward Beecher*

Your heart, O God, is warm and passionate, more powerful than the sun.

I cry out to you, O Lord, God of all. At night my thirsty soul cries out to you and I search for you, I long for you, I long for your presence. You've seemed closer than my skin, yet you're further than the stars. My flame has become a smouldering candle. Yet I rejoice before you, God. My Father, you've heard my cry. For you are a faithful God, even to me. Hold me, Dad. Hold me close, like a father holds his newborn baby, fragile and dependent. Praise the Lord, all you saints! Amen.

Lord, I want to thank you for the power of prayer. I had never been able to comprehend how praying helped, but I found out when prayers saved my life. Lord, for this reason and others I thank you with the whole of my heart.

Thank you so much for loving me and never stopping even when I deny you and make the wrong choices. You're so amazing, and knowing you're there for me is overwhelming. I'm so sorry for repeatedly letting you down and hurting you. I love you so much, Lord, even though I don't always show it. Thank you.

O my Father, thank you, Lord, for the many souls in this place. Thank you for your word, Lord, your word of life. Thank you for your precious cleansing blood and thank you for the gift of your son.

God in heaven, I thank you for the warmth and friendliness of the people around me. May your face shine on them as you watch over their comings and goings. May the love, warmth and friendship of heaven be near them. Now and always. Amen.

Lord, thank you for this place where we can gather together. It is a blessing that we can dwell in your presence. We pray that your Holy Spirit would refresh this space. Let us feel you, Lord. Lord Jesus, remember your promises – those that we hold dear and are so thankful for – that when we knock, the door will be answered to us. That you will never leave us. Thank you 4 prayer.

Lord God, thank you for the many amazing experiences that worshipping together gives us. Please let these experiences be connected with you. Thank you that you are patient and give us so many chances to meet with you in our lives. Please help us to make the most of these opportunities so that we can know you better and deal with life better. Thank you for always being with each of us always. Please let us be able to apply the things we learn here at other times when your presence is more apparent and take them with us to use in everyday life. Amen.

I thank U 4 UR faithfulness – for in times of doubt, trouble or fear U R there. When I run away, U run after me. Thank U 4 UR love, mercy, grace, understanding and promises, Lord! Amen.

Lord, the power of prayer is deep within us all. Help every person to praise your name and to come to realize how great you are. I want to focus wholly on you, Lord. Lord, hear me as I pray with everything I do given back to you as my humble offering.

Father, thank you for saving me when I cried out for help. I don't feel worthy of you; I prayed and you answered.

Thank you, Lord. I'm never going to be good enough for you but yet you tell me that you love me and I think that's amazing. I love you, even when I don't act like it. Help me do what you want me to do and guide me through to live life, shining your LOVE to those around me. Thank you for saving me. Lots of love, Rachel.

Hey, sometimes I feel lonely and I just want to say if others do too then talking to God really does work. When I'm scared I talk to Him and I don't feel scared anymore. It *is* amazing. I love you, God! Love, Lucy.

Dear Lord, I would like to thank U 4 coming into my life. Amen.

Lord, you do so much for us, but we take all your amazing gifts for granted. Help us to appreciate our gifts and to use them in this world.

Dear God, THANK YOU!!!!!!!!!!!!!!!!!!!!!!!!!!!!!! AMEN.

How dare I blame you for my mistakes and 4 stuff I do, U R perfect.

Lord, I thank you that your love is patient, your love is loud. It does not envy, it does not boast, it is not proud. It is not rude, it is not self-seeking, it is not easily angered, it keeps no record of wrong. Love does not delight in evil but rejoices with the truth. It always protects, always trusts, always hopes, always perseveres. Father, may I show this kind of love to you and others.

Dear God, our Father, Creator and Author, I place my faith in you to guide my life, I ask not for peace, I ask not for happiness, I ask not for pain, I ask not for joy. I ask not for sorrow, I only ask that you would show me your true way and help me know your true self the way you intended, whatever that may be. If this is what you intend. Amen.

O Lord our God, help us to love U with all our heart, with all our soul, with all our mind, and with all our strength!

Lord, you are the quiet power, the pulse of the universe is your heart beat. We see you everywhere in everything and so often we fail to see you anywhere. I have found you in the most unlikeliest places. You have met me in moments of despair, confusion, self-disgust, physical and psychological pain, guilt and grief. You have shown me you are greater than my inadequacy, stronger than the situation and people who oppress and frustrate me, more beautiful than all the glories of creation, and with a broader vision and wider embrace than my imagination can encompass. You are the Lord, the King, the creator God, you are my father, my mother, comforter and friend. You love me and this is a miracle surpassing all others. I am yours and I am still yours, I recommit myself to you and your purposes. I have kicked and struggled and cried and worn myself out, not wanting or meaning to rebel, but not understanding. And praying all the while, giving it all back to you, yet still feeling the anger and pain and not knowing what I should do. And in the middle of this fight with myself and my surroundings, you have intervened through a tragedy, and shown me love. Who am I then to fret about my own purposes, when yours are so clear, what does it matter who I am and where I go? Unless your love follows me and goes before me, hems me in, refuses to leave me alone, demands to be shared, pushes me onwards, guides me, forgives me. You will not let me go and I know this, deep inside me where there are no words.

Lord, I can't wait for the day when you will return and take us to heaven with you. That day of immense Glory and Victory over evil and death. I can't believe that we will be there; it's mind blowing. We will actually experience the glory and power and wonder of your return; we will see you at last. It's almost unbelievable because we don't deserve it. The only reason we will always be with you, saved from condemnation which we deserve, is because you paid the price for us. You died on the Cross, you were abandoned by your father, and you entered the world of evil where you fought for every one of us with such passion because you love us so much. The reason we are saved is due to your love, which is so infinite that we cannot fully understand it. And now I want to say thank you, but how?

What thanks can possibly be worthy of the deed? Thank you seems too simple and too easy to say, but it's all I can offer in words. But I can say thank you with my life, and that is what I want to do. I give you my life, I place it in your hands, you can do what you want with me. It is all I can give. Thank you that you have suffered for me. I'm gutted to think that it was my sin that forced you to the Cross. But I know that I'm forgiven, although I cannot understand that either. Thank you that I am saved, and help me to live my life with you every day. Amen.

PART TWO

Prayers for when it's just you and God

2

You and me, Lord

I have had prayers answered – most strangely so sometimes – but I think our heavenly Father's loving-kindness has been even more evident in what He has refused me. *Lewis Carroll*

Lord Jesus,
Into your arms I place my life,
Please live in me and teach me what is right when I stray
from your path. Amen.

Put your arms around me, Lord,
Hold me tight and true.
Rest my head upon your shoulder,
Point out what I must do.
Put your fingers on my lips, Lord.
Hold my tongue, it's sharp and quick.
Never let me think of speaking
Until your words are on my lips.

At the Cutting Edge

Lord,
Use me, I am willing,
I just wanna work 4 U!
Put me in the Church,
Where U want me 2 be,
Just use me!
Thanks 4 all you've done.
Some PPL say U don't exist,
But don't they look around and C wot U have done!
U R amazing!
THX 4 being an awesome guy. Amen.

I want to choose the narrow footpath
If it can somehow mean knowing you
– in radical no compromise.
Put a hold on this soggy comprising child so that nothing
on earth matters as much as knowing you.

Love is more than just a word, my child.
I hold you in my arms. Amen.

Lord, please look out for me as I start the next chapter
of my life at university. I believe you put me on this
path and I look forward to fulfilling my destiny as seen

in your eyes and written by your hand. Thank you in anticipation. Amen.

It's the narrow road you call us to, Lord, which is smelly, uncomfortable, ragged, demanding and at times painful and sacrificial, but amazingly exciting for those who choose to take up the Cross.

I'm a 'Peter', Lord, like on the Mount of Transfiguration, I want to set up a shelter for the pair of us away from this nasty sinful world. There it's cosy, safe and doesn't interfere with or challenge my worldly appetite for things and possessions.

Yet something inside wants to live on the edge, knowing what it is to taste holy fear.

To experience the risk of deep trust, and the exhilaration of knowing and loving God.

That's more than mere walking, it is real life embracing.

Let me go back to those God encounters – where nothing else in the world mattered more than serving and loving you. Amen.

Lord, Help me stand up 4 all that I believe . . .

I pray for everybody I know that isn't a Christian, especially my family. Help them know how truly amazing you are. I pray also for myself. Just help me to be what you want me to be and to put U 1st always. I love U, but it doesn't always show to others. Help it to. Thank you.

Why do I feel so much pain in my heart? Always there, never budging no matter what I do. I can't handle it. I look to God; is he there? He doesn't care about me, he's nothing special! All these horrible questions – I hate myself! But then I realize from somewhere – GOD LOVES ME! Really! Truly! Peace of mind, God loves me, I love God!

Lord, I pray that you will give us your strength and love 2 follow you daily and lose our lives for you. Live in us all and help us 2 always stand 4 what we believe in. Amen.

God – I wanna pray, firstly THANK U. I cannot begin till I thank U 4 the Cross, 4 Jesus' love, 4 forgiveness that I receive undeservingly but thankfully. Through Grace I am what I am. I'm here, Lord – thank U. Lord, I'm grateful for the opportunities I've been blessed with but I feel lost, Lord, with what 2 do with my future – confused – I want 2 do what U want me 2 do, but I'm scared.

Scared of a challenge of not hearing U, or thinking I do and getting it wrong. Lord, I pray U can show me the path to take.

Lord, I pray 4 my mum. Please let her see your love. Thank you that you have got a time when she will turn 2 U. I thank you that I know your will, but give me patience, love and forgiveness. And I pray, use me, Lord, in all of my life. What do I do? Tell me where I should go. Amen.

Dear God, thank you for changing my life. I'm not sure where I'd be now without you. Please stay with me and help me feel your presence in my hardest times.

Lord, I don't understand so much.
I am angry, lost, confused.
And yet I still feel your love, support and help.
What's going on?
Is it me?
Tell me the answer to the mystery!!
I need 2 know.
I need to hear U.
Please.

Dear Lord,
I pray 4 so many things, but mainly that U B with those in need.
Though I have problems and need UR guidance I know U R wid me.
But those who do not know UR love B wid them.

Lord, I know that you know the prayers in my heart and for that I thank you.

Thank you for the opportunities you have given me. I know that you have a plan for me. This make me very happy and that most of all you love me! I dedicate all that I do to you. Amen.

Jesus, where are you when my mind is struggling against my soul? I'm too tired to think and weeping comes like breathing. Everything is not alright. Jesus, please bring your living waters while I still have the strength to drink.

Lord, sometimes I feel lost and sometimes I feel confused and hurt. Lord, I pray that you teach me how to follow you and focus my life entirely on you. Help me to never stray from your path and help me to find and know you and live in your presence. Please help me in my search. Lead me to your love, help me to find you. But mostly, Lord, I want to say THANK YOU. Thank you for never leaving me and never giving up on me. Thanks for always loving me, I surrender my heart and life to you, Lord. I love you! Amen.

Father, as each day goes by we realize how much we need you and your forgiveness and your hope and your love. Thank you.

My life is in your hands, Lord, use me to be like you in my everyday life. Amen.

I am the little child with a snotty nose and a grazed knee and tears in my eyes!
You are the big Daddy who wipes my nose, cleans the dirt and gravel from my wound and wipes my eyes and kisses me better. Thank you!!!

My Father, your Glory covers the whole earth and your love is so very special. I thank you with all my heart, O God, for you have taken all my sins, all my addictions, all my unforgiveness and hurt and bore it upon the Cross at Calvary.

Father, make me a new person shaped in your image and filled with your love. Amen.

Dear Lord, time out.

Time out to be still.

Apart from the pressures of live and love and the dilemmas of the future.

Time out for myself – time into you.

Into the eternal purposes of the eternal God.

Help me to see your face.

The beauty of holiness.

The power of truth and justice.

Help me to get strength from spending time out with you.

Amen.

Lord Jesus, help us to help everyone believe you love them so very much. Amen.

I need to feel better about myself so that I will be less depressed and feel more loved.

God, I don't understand what you're doing in my life, help me have your peace.

Lord, I want to get to know you and love you as I have seen so many of my friends do. Please be with me – I want to love you as much as you love me. Amen.

Lord, I pray for a fairer and better life for all people who live in poverty, for whatever reason.

I pray that old scars will heal.

O Lord, my God from whom I have run as I have run from myself. Kiss me again with your truth, replace the innocence I can no longer feel with something greater and more precious.

Father, please give me the strength and opportunities to talk to my friends about your everlasting love. And I pray that more Christians would come 2 our area – please can my Christian friends become more open to talk about deep things. I need more people who I can trust. Please Father, Amen.

Lord, I want and need you more than anything else in this world. I focus too much on the materialistics, Lord – I feel troubled and unsure of myself when I let this happen, so Lord, please control me. Hold my hand – stop me from reaching out to wrong – to evil, to the devil. Lord help me to live my life in the purity of your kingdom. To be washed clean by your Holy Spirit – to know that by your blood I am saved – eternally.

Lord, I devote myself wholly to you because you and you alone are what I want. No evil – I want to be pure. I know that I am your precious child, Lord, but I need to commit myself to you more fully – no more 'Christian when it suits' business. I want to be me – who I am, no compromises. I want to stop hiding you to other people because, Lord, I know that your light, strength and power is there inside me, waiting to burst out and shine through me to others in this world. Lord, help me to be the witness to others that I know I can be. But, Lord, I need to remember to always focus on you because you are the most amazing thing that's ever happened to me. I want that amazing sense of presence, peace and power in my life every single day. I want you to be my best friend, my comfort, my strength and my guide.

Lord, you face me with new challenges every day. Some are tiny – and may be no more than a smile at someone I may not like, or that needs you. Others may be massive – such as leading worship. But, Lord, each and every one of these tasks were set before me by you! Help me to see that, Lord, you set them – so you help me through, building me up as you fill me with your Holy Spirit. Lord, I want to experience you more at these times. I pray that you are always there, but I am often cold-hearted and stubborn to acknowledge your presence. I am not worthy of all that you have done for me. Just the thought of you fills me with excitement and joy, but also fear.

Lord, I sometimes am unsure of how to approach you. Help me to break down these barriers because, Lord, I don't want anything to come between you and me. I want to be intimate with you, Lord. I want to love you so deeply my heart melts for you. Not saying that it doesn't already, because it does, and has, but, Lord, I want more. I want to be overwhelmed by your power. I feel dry and thirsty and I'm longing to feel your touch again. Lead me through my uncertainty of where in your house I belong. Help me to know where I am wanted and where I belong. I know you have your mind over this situation, Lord, but at the moment I'm really struggling to feel it. I seem to find myself in awkward situations, cold to your presence and lost for the power, words and actions to get me through. Lord, help me to feel your touch. Amen.

Lord, I know I do wrong, but I know you will forgive me. I know I lie and say bad things, but I know you will forgive me. I know you are listening, I know you are watching me, everything I do, there is nowhere to hide and run away from you. I know I can talk to you anytime, I love you so, but just promise me that you will not let me go.

God, I don't know where I am with you, but I know I'm not as close as I could be or want to be. Help me put aside everything that is getting in the way of being open with you.

Dear Lord, Let your light reach into the darkness and touch those who are in need of your love. Amen.

Dear Lord, help me through my exams. Please be there with me and guide me through. I'm so worried.

Dear God, please give us peace on earth and help everyone to love one another.

Lord, I pray that I will be more radical in my Christian discipleship, and live it out more and not be afraid of what people will say.

I want to come closer to God, he's the only one who can heal my brokenness and show me who I really am 'cos I don't know anymore.

3

For when you have questions

Call on God, but row away from the rocks. *Indian Proverb*

Why God? I feel so confused, so trapped, so alone. I know you are there and yet I perceive myself as bumbling along – just going along not quite knowing where. So our marriage is over. I'm relieved, yes relieved, I'm relieved. The pain is he never seemed to want to connect with me. He was cruel, mean and rejecting, belittling and ridiculing my family, my beliefs and things I hold dear to me. Whatever I tried to set up he seemed to sabotage. Overtly encouraging, covertly undermining, tap, tap, tapping away at my confidence, till it didn't exist anymore.

He hated/hates my vulnerability. Treating me and my children with contempt and punishment until we are shamed into becoming self-sufficient. Denying our neediness, our wants, our desires. My children are damaged, scarred forever by this wonderful, sensitive, charismatic man who appears to the outside world as the perfect husband and devoted father. I want to scream, 'It's not true!' – but it is, to him, to the people who perceive him this way. Oh God, what a mess, why, why, why? I cannot believe he is an evil person, a bad man, and yet he has hurt us all and perhaps himself too much.

Oh God, my children, my beautiful children – have I let them down by staying so long, colluding, perhaps even condoning his attitudes and behaviour? I feel so small, so inadequate, so guilty, so unsure. I feel that he is my thorn in the flesh, my malignant disease that with constant vigilance can be kept in check but ultimately can turn up unexpectedly in shockingly undefended places.

As I write this he sounds so big, so powerful yet he isn't. He is a man, just a man. He has few friends – none who seem to engage with him, or him with them, on a level deeper than his chosen profession. 'Selling the dream.'

My heart feels crushed and broken. Seventeen years down, the rest of our human lives to be irretrievably connected to each other, and when we die our children will bear the scars of our futility. I don't understand, I feel so small, but I know you are there and even though I don't understand, I trust you implicitly.

Lord Jesus, sometimes I doubt, sometimes I'm tempted, sometimes I deliberately turn my back and choose to go the other way. Sometimes I can't be bothered with you, sometimes I'm ashamed. You know my all, you know, Lord, what's going on in my head and heart – you know when I feel lonely, you know when I yearn to pray and read your word and sing your praise. You know my needs and you satisfy them fully. You are faithful – keeping your promises – answering my prayers. Lord God, I want to renounce everything I hold dear which is of this world – all the sin that so easily entangles. Lord, be king over everything. I give you all that is in my life – my family, work, friends, relationships, food, clothes, money, CDs, uni work, church – Jesus, you are MORE IMPORTANT than any of these – have your place as king of my life – reigning over everything and lead me, Lord, guide me as you promise. Thank you that you have chosen me to be your servant – Lord, teach me to serve. In Jesus' name. Amen.

4

For when you are anxious for the future or have important decisions to make

Prayer does not change God but it changes him who prays. *Søren Kierkegaard*

Dear God, thinking about the future can be so daunting. On the one hand we're full of all the possessions we're going to acquire and the places we're going to see. And there is all the uncertainty about jobs, careers and domestic life. Guide us and help us choose the right path to go.

Dear God, the future is getting nearer and I'm getting more afraid. Exams are important. What if I fail? What will I do in life? In ten years' time where will I be? Not only are we afraid of our own future, but the future of the world. We're destroying your creation out of greed. Our environment is very important yet we're killing it. Help us, Lord, and guide us towards renewing your world. Amen.

Jesus, I know you are there at all times, loving me and protecting me. Thank you that my destiny is planned and you're always in control of my life. Thank you that in times of trouble, hurt and need, you are standing with your arms open wide, ready to hold and comfort me. You're the only thing in my life I can depend on to be there at all times, ready to pick up the pieces when my life seems in shatters. I love you so much. Please guide me along the path you want me to go. In your name. Amen.

Dear Lord, thank U 4 being with me in all that I do. Guide me so that I find the right road. Help me to be more understanding to other people's problems.

Heavenly Father, send me out into the world in the power of your Holy Spirit to work for you, to strive for peace and to complete the task you have set for me. I sometimes worry about the future but I'll try to trust you as much as I can. Reassure me when I doubt and correct me when I stray. I know I'm here for a purpose, so please let me fulfil that. Amen.

Dear Lord, help us 2 B confident and have courage towards obstacles in the future. Please guide us in the right way and help us to avoid bad temptations. We have to try not to fill ourselves with anxiety and to put on a brave face as we face the uncertainty of the future. We must try to remember that you're with us all the way.

Dear Father, as time draws on and our love for you extends, help us deal with life in troubled times, so that our love for you wins through. May the future be bright and happy so that we can celebrate your love and care. Give us faith to trust in you, for we are your children. Amen.

When I'm scared of the future, comfort me and let me know that U R there all the way.

Lord, we have to make many choices and decisions in our lives, some more important than others. Guide us in the right way to make the best decisions.

Heavenly Father, I pray that you'll guide me as I make this important decision. Let me put all trust in you and follow your lead in whichever direction it takes me.

Strengthen me with your Spirit after the decision is made, so that I feel sure that I'm following your will, especially if I'm not really sure that the right decision has been made. In Jesus' name. Amen.

5

For when relationships are difficult at home

> In prayer, it is better to have heart without words, than words without heart. *John Bunyan*

Dear God, we know that sometimes we argue with our parents because they've said or done something we don't agree with. Help us to try and see their point of view and to see how difficult being a parent is.

Dear Father God, when I need guidance and I'm in trouble please help me through. I know when troubles and arguments occur in my family you're there to help. When I fall out with friends and feel lonely, you're there to help. When work seems endless and worthless, you are there to help. I thank you, Lord, for always being there to help. But please guide me to help those who have problems big and small. Amen.

At the Cutting Edge

Dear God, sometimes it is difficult for us to appreciate the love and care of our parents, especially when we are not allowed to do something. Help us understand that our parents are trying to guide us through the bad things in life and to help us deal with everyday problems. Father, help us to understand this when we are feeling down. Thank you, God.

Lord, I thank you for parents. I thank you that they *do* know what's best for us, however many times we think otherwise, and that they are always there to support and encourage us. Father, I pray that we'll realize how much our parents do love us, and how much they are prepared to do for our well-being. I pray, Lord, for the times when things aren't going well, that we will learn from the experience and grow to love and respect our parents more. Amen.

Please be with people who R finding life at home hard and distressing. Pour UR love over them, so that they can love each other.

'Honour your parents', that's what the Bible says. But at the moment I just can't stand them. Why can't they understand how I feel and see my point of view? If only they would stop getting at me. But, Lord, you ask me to love them no matter what they're like. It seems you're my only hope of doing that at the moment! Help me make the effort to understand their way of thinking and to be patient. And help me control my big mouth, because I say things I really don't mean and I start shouting.

Lord Jesus, I come to you for forgiveness for not being obedient to my parents. It's really hard not to fly off the handle when they stop me from doing things. Help me to honour them both, and by your Spirit join us in family love so that we can work things out peacefully. Amen.

Dear Lord, help me realize that when I argue with my parents, they are only trying to help. Give me consideration for them, and give them wisdom and knowledge to do what is best for me.

6

For when someone lets you down

Prayer is not asking. It is a longing of the soul. It is daily admission of one's weakness. *Mahatma Gandhi*

Dear God, I know you're my best friend and that you'll never let me down. You're always there when I need someone to talk to. But why aren't my friends the same? They sometimes won't talk and sometimes I feel they don't respect my belief in you. All I ask is that they may find friendship and understanding through you. Also, please forgive us all for the wrong things we do.

Heavenly Father, you know I've been let down. Lord, help me overcome my feeling of despair and try to continue with my life as normal. Father, thank you for never letting me down and for letting me come to you in times of trouble. I pray that my trust will be fully in you during this difficult time. In Jesus' name. Amen.

When someone lets U down you can forget that God is there. You sulk and think U R on your own. Dear Lord, help us not to sulk but to turn to U when things go wrong.

Dear Lord, help me be strong. I've been let down by my friend. Let me try and forgive them and not do the same back through spite. Help us keep our friendship even if we let one another down. Amen.

Dear God, thank you for being my friend. Please help me understand that other people aren't as perfect as you and can't always be what I want them to be. Please help me be a friend to others that they can depend on and trust.

Dear Father, help me forgive other people when they hurt me and let me say sorry when I'm wrong. Help me to admit my mistakes when I don't get on with friends and parents. Please give me happiness when I'm depressed, company if I'm lonely and peace if I'm angry. Amen.

Dear Father, help!

Lord, help me remember that when someone lets me down you'll always be with me, and if I do wrong, you'll always be ready to welcome me back.

Dear Lord, I've been let down. I know I should forgive them, but I find it hard as I've been hurt by someone I trust. I know I've also let people down and I ask you to forgive me. Help me forgive the people who have let me down so that we can build our trust and friendship with one another. Amen.

Heavenly Father, help us when our friends let us down, may we always remember that *you* will never do that.

Dear God, I often feel so annoyed and angry when my friends let me down. I feel lonely and unwanted. Why are they ignoring me, what have I done? Lord, it's hard to forgive. But then I remember how many times I ignore you. Yet you're not bitter, Lord, you still love and forgive me. I'm always letting you down, Lord, and I know how you must feel deep down, lonely and unwanted.

Yet you're always there for me when I need you. Dear Lord, I'm sorry for neglecting you, and I pray you'll give me strength to love you more each day. Amen.

Oh Lord, thanks that you never leave us, no matter how hard life gets or how far I feel from you; you're always there by my side. Lord, help me rely on you, and put my trust in your constant love. You alone will never let me down or desert me in times of trouble. But Lord, let me forgive those friends who fail me when I need them most. Lord, don't let me grow bitter or resentful but renew our love and deepen our friendship. Lord, thanks for your unfailing love for me. Amen.

7

For your enemies

We may pray most when we say least, and we may pray least when we say most. *St Augustine of Hippo (AD 354–430)*

Lord, I pray that in this world of hate, when someone hurts me in one way or another, you'll give me the strength and the sense of mind to turn the other cheek and forgive. Also when someone thinks of me as an enemy, I ask you to help me love them back. Amen.

Dear Lord, help us not 2 think wrongly of others. Help us see that they too have people they find hard 2 get on with. Help us turn wrong 2 right and join in with others.

Dear Lord, help me when friends tease me and wind me up, so that I don't lose my temper and say things that could hurt. Help me show that same love you give to me.

Dear Lord, we pray for all our enemies, the people we don't particularly like or get on with and who stress our nerves. Help us be more friendly towards them and not exclude them in any way. In Jesus' name. Amen.

Dear God, please help me be a friend to my enemies and help me be nice to them even if they're horrible to me.

Dear Lord, help us see the beauty in all people and not judge a person by their appearance. Amen.

Lord, help us think before we react. Help us think about others and not just ourselves. Make us understand how others feel instead of abusing them to make us feel better. Lord, in your mercy, hear our prayer. Amen.

Holy Father, draw my enemies closer to U.

Dear Lord, please help me get on with other people. Help me see their point of view, especially when it's different from my own. Help me consider others' advice, and help me to ask for it when I'm unsure. Let them know they can trust me, and help me learn to trust them.

Lord, it's hard to be with people, it's difficult to communicate. It's not easy to love, care and respect others. Sometimes we try too hard, sometimes we give up altogether. Lord, we know you'll always love us so we may learn to love each other. Amen.

PART THREE

Prayers for when you are thinking of others

8

Thinking of others

There are thoughts which are prayers. There are moments when, whatever the posture of the body, the soul is on its knees. *Victor Hugo*

I hold in your presence, Lord, a friend of mine.
She has a mixed up head.
She needs to see your light shining on the answer to her problems.
Help her to be strong throughout this tough part of her life.
Help her overcome her sadness and disillusionment of the world.
Hold her in your hands and breathe your Holy Spirit into her.
Through Jesus. Amen.

Pray 4 all those who struggle with loneliness, depression, paranoia and other such problems.
Pray that they will find refuge and stability and healing.
Amen.

Dear God, please bring my family together and stop them from arguing.

Lord, help my friends who are refugees. They need a church where they can worship you safely. They are only young – they need someone to show them the way because even though they have the best intentions there are so many temptations for them. Help them to get over the war and violence they have seen. They have suffered so much and seem so much older than their years. Please give them a little of their childhood back. May they always continue to love and work with your children who have been rejected in their country. Please bless this work and allow them to continue the improvements that were so drastic even from the beginning. May they always know your love and let their little lights shine. Build your kingdom there through them. Amen.

Dear Lord,
I pray for my friends,
All who search and would love to find your presence.
Whatever you may have planned for their lives,
I pray they may feel your guidance so strongly.

In faith I ask for your blessing on their lives,
And trust that you may show them some of the delight
you have blessed me with. In Jesus' name. Amen.

Dear Lord Jesus,
I really pray that U may bless my friends who I name
before you now.
(*Pause and quietly name them all as part of your prayer.*)
Fill them with your Holy Spirit and let them know that
your love is unconditional.
Please, Father. Amen.

Lord, I pray for my friends, that they can find space in
their hearts for you.
I pray that they will find you and learn to love you,
always.
Thank you that you do care for my friends.

Dear God, I pray that U will help all those who come
from broken homes.
For those who don't know their dad, or have problems
at home.
Bring healing to their lives and help their dads live up
to their responsibilities.

Lord, for AIDS and HIV orphans and those with the disease, may they not be ignored and may help come when they need it.

I pray 4 my Christian friends wandering from U or not focusing on U or not putting U at the centre of their lives.
U R the centre – the key 2 life.

Lord, why?

Lord, I pray for my friends who struggle with being a Christian. May they learn that it is OK to question their faith, and may they realize there are some things there is no easy answer to. But may they feel your Holy Spirit in their hearts and know that through all the suffering and turmoils of life they can always rely on you. Amen.

Lord, I pray for those without Jesus who don't know just what He has to offer – the love and grace and mercy.

Lord, please mend the broken hearts, kiss UR crying children back to life and show them UR love.

Lord, my parents aren't getting on any longer and things are getting worse.
I pray that they will see that they need 2 make a greater commitment 2 U.

Lord, my friends don't know your love,
I pray that they will surrender to your loving embrace.
Show them that drink, drugs and sex cannot fulfil their appetite.
Replace these desires with a want to know you more.
Lord, give them a vision of your reality.
Help them seek and knock and then I pray that their hearts may be ready to accept you as their Lord and Saviour. Amen.

Lord, I pray for those who are confused and who don't know where or who to turn to. Amen.

For all my friends that they will not be led into bad ways.

I pray that you could help my mum find the strength to give up smoking. She tries so hard to stop yet never reaches her goal. Lord, give her the courage to stop and the will to never pick one up again. Thank you, Lord. Amen.

I pray for my friends (*name them before God, thinking of an attribute that you are especially thankful for*), and all the rest I have forgotten for being such great friends and being there for me. I hope they all find love, warmth and happiness!

Lord help my sister be happy after a very sad hard time. Help my mum be happy even though her life makes her sad sometimes. Let my dad come home. Thank you.

Dear God, thank you for my grandad. I feel that I owe him so much. I know that we didn't talk much, but he inspired me so much. The amount of hope he showed made me so happy and proud to be a part of his life. I'm sorry we didn't talk much, but because we didn't this has made me feel the need to talk to you God and so through his death I have been brought closer to you. It seems as though there could be an answer to everything, if we only looked. My grandad managed to touch so many lives even when suffering from a stroke, and that makes me so proud to have been a part of his life. He was such an inspiration. I loved him. I never got the chance to say it to him but I mean it and have always done so. We will meet again some time but until then, thank you God, for grandad. I hope I make him proud of me in the same way I am of him.

Dear Lord, please help all the people who have lost loved ones through violence or war.
I pray especially for——who is feeling very sad.

Please pray for the family of my friend——who died recently at such a young age. Look after his/her family as they come to terms with their grief.

9

For when you or your friends feel sad or down

> Prayer is not an old woman's idle amusement. Properly understood and applied it is the most potent instrument of action. *Mahatma Gandhi*

Lord, you know that as teenagers we are changing from children to adults. Our emotions are unreliable and change depending on our mood. When we're in a mood of depression and cannot 'snap out of it' help us feel that you are there with us. Touch us with your Holy Spirit so that we feel happy again. Amen.

Dear Lord, this is a small prayer when my friends or I feel sad. I know that when we're sad we need to talk to someone about it and it is not always easy. I'd like to thank you that although I can't always talk about some things with my friends I know you will always be there for me.

Father, I thank you that you are always with us and will never let us down. Sometimes life seems really difficult, and there are no easy answers to our problems. I thank you that you understand what we go through, and that you can support and help us. Enable us to give all our problems over to you and trust in your answers. Through Jesus' name. Amen.

Lord, at the moment everything I do seems to be wrong. Whatever I turn my hand to doesn't go according to plan. Why is life so difficult? Please Lord, help me through this difficult patch. Each day guide me along the pathway and give me grace. Help me to be brave and to remember that I'm much more fortunate than many others. In your name. Amen.

Dear God, help us 2 get on with our friends and 2 forgive them if they hurt our feelings.

Lord, when I'm unhappy, pick me up. When I'm losing faith, show me the path to your love. When I'm upset, help me get through it, and when I'm happy, rejoice with me. Amen.

Jesus, I'm really depressed. Why did it have 2 happen 2 me? I may have made a mess of things, but I didn't really deserve it. Or did I Lord?

Dear Lord, there are times when we feel that everything is against us, when we feel that no one appreciates us or cares. These times make us feel alone, insecure and unhappy. But Lord, you are always there to help us and love us and you never turn your back even when we sin. Help us feel your presence, Lord, at times like this and to love and appreciate you. Thank you. Amen.

Dear Lord, help those who feel sad or down, for people who worry over things large and small. Let them know U are always there whenever they need you.

Dear Lord, when we are feeling depressed help us remember all the wonder of your creation, the delicate creatures you have created and the awesome landscape of the world. And above all, Lord, remind us of the everlasting love you have shown us. In God's name.

I have friends, Lord, whom I love so much. They are hurt, confused, mixed up, frightened and angry. How can I help them? What can I do? They need love and understanding. They need you. They are crying out for help. They cry out for love but there is no one there – except you. Help me show your love to them and ease their pain. Amen.

10

For those doing exams

A man is powerful on his knees. *Corrie Ten Boom (1892–1983)*

Dear Lord, please be with me when I'm in the exam room. sitting at my desk, writing away. Please help me, Lord.

Dear God, at this time I ask you to stand by me while I take my exams. When I get nervous, calm me down. When I get upset, help me remain happy. And, Father, help me realize that you are always there for me to turn to. Amen.

Dear Lord, the pressure of exams can be daunting and stressful – it seems like a never-ending tunnel of darkness. Help us realize that you are the light of the world and that your love always shines in us. We can only do our best, so help us realize that this is good enough for you.

Dear Lord, when we're preparing for exams and taking them we feel they'll never end and that what we do is never enough. Help us realize that exams are not the most important thing in life and that you will lead us the way you want us to go, even if this means being disappointed with the results at the time. Thank you that you're always there when we need you. Amen.

I can't wait to finish the exams, Lord. When I get the results back please give me UR peace, no matter what they're like. Don't let me forget that you'll never leave me and that UR love for me has got nothing to do with how I do in the exams.

Dear Lord, I know you're there watching over me all the time, guiding me through good and bad times, giving me strength to do all that I do. I ask you, Lord, especially to help me throughout my exams when I need you most. Help me persevere through to the end, give my best performance and keep calm at all times. Thank you, Lord. Amen.

God don't let my exams take your place; help me to keep them in perspective and realize that it's all under control.

Father, thank you for the opportunity to learn and gain knowledge. In this trying period of exams, please help me do my best, but not crowd you and others close to me out of my life with work. Help me not to be disappointed with my results and not to reject those who have not done as well as I have. I ask this through your Son. Amen.

Dear Lord, please guide me through this time of exams. Help me be calm throughout and work to my best ability. Strengthen me as I do last-minute revision so that I can achieve the results I deserve. Lord, I know you will be with me in these exams, guiding my mind in the right direction. Help me know you will always be with me.

11

For those coping with family breakdown

> **Do not pray for easy lives. Pray to be stronger men and women.** *John F. Kennedy*

Lord, don't let people be worried about talking to you and asking you for help. When my parents divorced, my world caved in for months. I was scared of asking you for help in case I sounded selfish. But you never let me down. Even now I need to talk to you about my parents. It seemed you were the only one who cared about me. But you taught me to trust and love my parents again. Thank you, for ever.

Lord, we pray for those going through divorce, and coping with the hurt and rejection it brings. Give them courage and strength in their hour of need, and give them hope for the future. We pray that you'll help them, that they'll always have you and your everlasting love. Amen.

Lord, when my parents split up, I felt lost, unloved, alone. I felt that for some reason it was my fault. I thank U that although some may fall in and out of love, UR love is everlasting, however bad I feel.

Lord, we pray for all those going through the pain of divorce, especially we pray for the children of the families as they see their parents argue because of the friction caused by the long legal process. Give them the strength to carry on. Give parents self-control so that the divorce can be settled peacefully, and give strength to other married couples to carry on through troublesome times. In Jesus' name we ask this. Amen.

I can't believe it, Lord. My parents are divorcing! Help me, please God, through this troubled time. Believe me, I need it.

Father, please help and support children whose parents are coming to terms with divorce. Help the children realize that it's not their fault, and that both their mother and father love them and need their support. Amen.

Lord, it's hard to cope when families break up. Often it's the children of the marriage who feel most let down. Please help all children, and indeed adults in these situations to know that U will never let them down and that U will be with them always.

Dear Lord, although you put together many families, some of them split up and it can leave hatred and anger. We just ask that you'll help the parents and children involved in a divorce. Please be with them and help them in this time of distress and trauma. Please calm everyone and help them to get over it and lead their everyday lives again. Amen.

PART FOUR

Prayers for those who are suffering

12

For the sick

The man who says his evening prayer is a captain posting his sentinels. He can sleep. *Charles Baudelaire*

Lord, we pray that those who are sick can find healing in your love, that those who are lonely can find friendship in your care, and that those who feel lost can return to your knowledge. But most of all, Lord, we pray that those who are sad can find contentment in your presence. In Jesus' name.

Father, we ask that you'll give strength and peace to those who are in any way burdened by physical or emotional pain. Help them in their time of need, give others around them compassion and patience to bear witness to them when they are sharing Christ's pain. Lord, we ask this in Jesus' name. Amen.

Lord, very often we only think and pray for ourselves. Please help us pray for those less fortunate. We forget there are those who are sick at home and in hospital. We pray that you'll look after them and help us all during difficult times.

Dear God, help us give thanks for the people who care for us, the hard-working doctors and nurses who make the world a better place to live in. We thank you for our family and friends who care for us when we're ill. Amen.

Lord, give strength 2 those who are ill, especially those who are terminally ill and know that they don't have long 2 live. Let them turn 2 U for help.

Dear Lord, we pray for all who are sick and needy, especially those with terminal illnesses. May their sorrow and that of their families be calmed by the knowledge that they'll soon enter your eternal kingdom to be with you. Help them through their last days on earth so that they may not suffer. For the love of your only son whose suffering was long. Amen.

Lord, in your great glory and mercy please help all those who suffer sickness or pain, especially those close to us. We ask you to be present with those who are terminally ill. Father, give them all your strength, love and peace of mind.

Dear God, please help all the sick and needy people in this world, along with the old people we tend to forget about. Also the homeless and the people with personal problems at home. Amen.

Lord, help those who are sick, help us 2 help them get better, and make us care for those who R sick. Even if we're worried about our own health, give us strength 2 pick them up when they R down. Keep all those who R sick in good faith.

13

For those who are disabled

> Work as if you were to live a hundred years. Pray as if you were to die tomorrow. *Benjamin Franklin*

Lord, help us treat disabled people like ourselves. Though they face many problems and their lives are restricted, they're the same as us inside.

Dear Father, we know you love us all, but sometimes it's hard to remember. Let us try to love everyone around us. Help us especially to love those with a physical or mental disability. Let our love guide them towards you because in you we all become stronger and more loving servants. Teach those who are blind to the qualities of handicapped people that they can love them too. Amen.

Prayers for those who are suffering

Dear Lord, help those who are disabled and find life difficult. Bless and guide all those who look after them.

Lord, help those who are disabled, give them the strength to try new things and to help others. Also, Lord, help us not to see people who are handicapped as different, but remind us that they are people too. Amen.

Dear God, help those who are disabled cope with their disabilities and encourage people 2 support them and not turn away.

Lord God, please help me look upon myself not as disabled but different. Help me overcome the sadness I may feel and know that U are with me always.

14

For those with drug and
alcohol addiction

He who fails to pray does not cheat God. He cheats himself. *George Failing*

Dear lord, we pray for those who R either involved with drugs or who R finding it hard 2 resist drugs from so-called friends. Please give them strength 2 say, 'No!'

Lord, help those who take harmful drugs, like cocaine and heroin, overcome their addiction. Help them understand the harm it does. Give young people the wisdom to realize that drugs like nicotine have an effect on people later in life. Please make sure my family, friends and myself never feel the need to take drugs. Amen.

Lord, please help those who have drug and alcohol problems. Help them be strong and try 2 overcome their painful situation.

Lord, we pray for those who use or are tempted to experiment with drugs. We pray that they realize the danger of what they are doing. I ask you to give us the strength to help those we know who are on drugs, and to resist the temptation to take them ourselves.

God, give strength to those who abuse alcohol and drugs. Give them strength to see their mistakes. Many are homeless due to their addiction. I know it's hard for them to quit. Make them see all the worry and stress they are causing to their family and friends. Help them come to terms with reality and to see that life can have a deeper meaning. Help the dealers see how much damage and misery they are causing. For you are the only addiction of peace, love and hope. Amen.

Dear Lord, we pray 4 the many people in this world who are suffering with the problems of alcohol and drug addiction. Help them overcome their habits and support them in their hour of need.

Dear Lord, help me use my eyes as your eyes to help those who have drug and alcohol problems, and not to dismiss them but to commend them to you. Give me the courage to tell them what they are doing to themselves, and to show them there is a way out. I see my friends around me, Lord, doing things I know will harm them. Let me help them face their problems. Grant them the strength to fight. Amen.

15

For those suffering with AIDS

> No one is a firmer believer in the power of prayer than the devil; not that he practises it, but he suffers from it. *Guy H. King*

Lord, help all those suffering with AIDS. Help their families come to terms with what has happened and not to judge them. Help them live their lives to the full for however long they have left. Give them the strength to face the world and show them that your love never fails. Amen.

Jesus, you wouldn't be afraid to touch or love someone with AIDS. You'd invite them to your home and eat with them. You wouldn't judge them if they had sinned. Help me not to judge, help me not to feel scared, help me not to feel helpless. Give me strength to open my arms, my church, my home and my love to anyone who needs it. Help me be like you. Amen.

At the Cutting Edge

Heavenly Father, help those people suffering with AIDS. Make them strong and give them courage to carry on. We ask you, Father, that like other diseases, a cure will be found. Help those who suffer to tell others about the danger of this disease. We also pray for the families and friends in their times of sorrow and grief, that they will be able to comfort those who are dying. Support them in their hour of need. Amen.

Dear Lord, throughout the world there are many people who suffer from AIDS and the HIV virus. Often they have caught the disease through no fault of their own and are left weak and ill for the rest of their shortened lives. We pray that a cure is found for this horrific illness and that the suffering of many will soon end. For this we pray with all our hearts.

Heavenly Father, we pray 4 all the people in the world suffering from AIDS. We ask that U give them courage and determination 2 cope with the disease. We also ask that U comfort the families of all victims.

Lord, there are many things that people fear in our world, famine, war, poverty, homelessness – the list seems endless. But these things have all been around for many years and in some ways we understand them. But now we have a new fear which we cannot cope with and do not fully understand – AIDS. People who have AIDS don't have the support of knowing that the problem has been medically treated before. They must feel alone and insecure. Help them realize that you are always there for them and that you always care – and that we do as well. Amen.

Lord, we pray for those suffering with the HIV virus and for those living around them, be they friends or family. We pray they will have the help and support they need in times of hardship and illness. We pray for the doctors and nurses who help with the care of those with this illness and we pray for a speedy cure.

Lord, please help those people with AIDS or who are HIV positive. Help them in their pain and suffering, and let them know they are not alone in their grief. Please help ease the pain that their families are going through. Teach those who are ignorant about the disease that they need to give their love and not treat sufferers 'like lepers'. Help us learn more about AIDS so that we can find a cure soon and so put hope into the lives of those who suffer. Amen.

At the Cutting Edge

Lord God, U love us with a love that knows no limits. But we understand life only in part. In our pain, our anger and our fear, may we still find UR love, 4 U R the only rock we can cling 2 that will not let us down.

16

For those with incurable diseases

> Prayer is not a substitute for work, thinking, watching, suffering or giving; prayer is a support for all other efforts. *George Buttrick*

Father, please help those suffering with cancer. Sadly there are thousands today who are in pain due to this disease. Please give them help and love throughout their illness, and for those who will never recover please give them faith and trust in you. Amen.

Lord, please help people fighting against cancer. We all know it's a terrible disease. Please help them never 2 give up.

Lord, we pray for those who have cancer and who worry about what might happen to them. We ask you to calm their fears and let them know that you know their future and will always be with them. We ask this in your name.

Dear Lord Jesus, we pray for all those suffering from incurable diseases. You know what they are going through, as you experienced such pain on the Cross. Help them remember that you love them, since they may doubt your love for them, and fill them with your Holy Spirit and never-ending love. Amen.

Dear God, you show love in funny ways, sometimes taking the ones we love the most. Cancer – it's a horrid word, but many people have to cope with its consequences. Help us to deal with the pain and hurt it causes, because it is at these times that we need you most. Give us the strength to help others affected by it, and give us the right words and actions to comfort them. We need your help, God. Amen.

Lord, can U please give strength 2 those who R fighting against cancer. Help doctors find a cure so that people don't have 2 suffer.

Dear Lord, we pray for all the people who are suffering from cancer, whether curable or incurable. Help them live a good life during their ordeal, and if it is curable, to recover completely. If they're going to die, please let them die peacefully, and look after them in heaven. Amen.

17

For those who are bereaved

> Prayer is not a substitute for work, thinking, watching, suffering or giving; prayer is a support for all other efforts. *George Buttrick*

Dear Lord, when we are trying 2 cope with the loss of a loved one please give us strength 2 see it through and 2 realize that they have passed into UR hands, 2 a much better and happier place. Fill us with UR peace over this difficult period of time.

Dear Lord, it's difficult to cope when someone you love dies. It doesn't seem fair, we want to blame you, even though we know it's not your fault. They may no longer be in pain, but those of us left behind hurt deep inside. Though they may have entered an existence even more beautiful than life, the world seems dark and pointless to those who remain. So I ask you to help all those who cry for those they've loved and lost, so that they may continue to praise you and not lose faith. Amen.

Dear Lord, please help those who have lost a friend or member of their family. Let them remember that however sad they feel, U will always be there 2 love and care 4 them.

Dear Lord, give us strength in coping with death, the death of someone close 2 us. Give us confidence in U 2 know that you're looking after our loved ones. Thank you, Lord.

Dear Lord Jesus, when you lose a close friend it's so hard to accept. It's like it never happened, just some horrible nightmare. Oh God, so many questions. Why, what's the point? Why did you take away someone I love, someone so young who never even had a chance to live? When something like this happens it's so easy to become bitter and twisted. Life can become really hopeless. Why have you done this to me, why have you made so many people suffer? Please Lord Jesus, it's so easy to lose hope. Please use this situation and make it meaningful, so that it does not become just another dark area inside, something too painful and too difficult to face. Please use this situation so that their death is meaningful. Oh God, help me find a purpose so that my life can become real, meaningful and worth living. Amen.

Dear God, help those who R grieving for the loss of a loved one or friend. Be with them at this time and let them know they have gone 2 a better place.

Dear Lord, please help those who have lost someone close 2 them, and help them understand that their spirit lives on as strong as ever.

Dear Father God, when a friend or relative is dying they are scared of not knowing what tomorrow holds and where they are going. Please help them and us realize that they are leaving this world and going into your loving gentle caring hands. Please help those who grieve to grieve less, and those who weep to weep less, and those who don't understand why, to understand more. Amen.

18

For those who are outcasts in society

> The only time my prayers are never answered is on the golf course. *Billy Graham*

Lord, sometimes we feel left out and ignored by our friends after some silly quarrel, and we feel hurt and alone. Help us remember those who feel left out every day, left out by their friends, rejected by society, those for whom luck never seems to come their way. Thank you for the security of our homes and families, and we lift up to you those who tonight will not have a roof over their heads or somewhere to go home to. We remember them in the name of your son who was rejected by his people and often felt an outcast of society. Amen.

Father God, help all those who R rejected or outcast from our society, because of race, religion or appearance. Help us accept them and put aside any dislikes or prejudices, and view everyone in the same light.

Dear Lord, let us remember the quiet people. The ones who sit in the corner all alone. The ones who have no friends because they are a different colour or because they are strange. Let us remember those people and be kind to them.

Dear God, fill us with your Holy Spirit so that we may be active people for you in this hurting world. Give us strength to come alongside the downtrodden. Let your love flow through us so that we may comfort the outcasts in our society, and teach us humility so that we may put our arms around the unloved. Amen.

Please Lord, help those who R rejected in society for one reason or another. If people R prejudiced towards them give them strength 2 cope.

PART FIVE

Prayers for the wider world

19

For God's world

> **Every great movement of God can be traced to a kneeling figure.** *D. L. Moody*

God, U don't just love those who R perfect,
UR gospel and love R 4 all the world and all people!
No matter what they've done, said, felt or how bad they
think they R – allow yourself 2 love Him, lads!

Lord, we pray for the countries that are suffering famine at the moment. The causes seem to be more than just drought and crop failure, but are caught up with civil war, corruption, exploitation and incompetence. Help all government and voluntary agencies who are trying to bring emergency aid to those who are starving, and move me to contribute and do what I can for the relief of suffering. Amen.

Lord, shake the people of our country from their apathy.
Help them to be bothered about the things that bother
you.
Make them realize there is more to life than simply
looking good.

Philosophers search fruitlessly for the meaning of life.
Christians know it from the moment they know your
love in their hearts.
Thank you!

A child stands crying
Her mother weeps
Crimson stains creep once more
Down the cities narrow streets

A baying crowd
Nervous troops
of soldiers eying angry men
Fingers itching willing to shoot

Two thousand years have passed
And still
Envy and hatred stalk the streets
Behind weapons enforcing their will

A simple man
Whip-scarred and stained

Nail-pierced hands reach out
To every face contorted with pain

I cannot really understand
I don't know how they feel
But our God has been there too
And his blood-stained hands can heal.

Heavenly Father
Food for the starving
Comfort for those who are lonely
Medical expertise for those who are sick
Care and love for orphans
Compassion for us that we can pray for them
Through your precious Son, Jesus Christ. Amen.

Lord, what one earth have we done to your world?
Exploitation, oppression and starvation.
There has to be a better way.
Teach us, Lord, to seek the common good and look
beyond our own selfish gain.
Help us to speak out against injustice
And never be apathetic about the needs of the poor.
Amen.

Dear Lord, help us 2 find a solution 2 global warming and be more responsible 4 this beautiful earth U have given us.

Stop! Be what you are,
Not what the world wants you to be.
God made you.
We need to take care of what God has made,
Not continue the constant manipulation of who we are and what we look like.
You are a custodian of God's creation (you!) so treat yourself with respect.
You are a beautiful human person!

Let Jesus shine out thru us Christians so that thousands and millions more may see His love and follow him. Amen.

Father of all, I pray for everything that's bad in the world and hope that one day when U come again there will be no more war, hunger and homelessness.

Lord, I can't even begin to thank you as much as you deserve for all you do for us. Yet I have this terrible feeling of guilt and sadness when I see people in need. The ill, the poor, or those just hurting spiritually. I feel as though I should be doing something. I feel so lucky that I know of you and when I walk down the street and see drunks, druggies, the homeless, the depressed, my heart cries out to them to know your love. I want to do something and I know that my friends do as well.

So, Lord, please be with my friends and me while we do our outreach and help us not to be disheartened by the overwhelming need before us, for we are your army and we want to make your kingdom come.
Stay with us, but more importantly be with those that need you most, that need your comfort, your ear to listen to them, and for you to be their friend.
Thank you in advance. Amen.

Lord, this is your world, help us 2 change it for the better.

God, show us more of your heart for justice.
Shake us out of our comfort and forgive our selfishness.
Challenge us about what really matters.
Lord, how can I make a difference?
Lord, I want to be obedient to your will . . .

To spend myself on behalf of the poor and needy,
The broken and the voiceless.
Thank you for giving me so much. Amen.

I would like to pray for everyone who feels alone and unhappy but is not asking for help, whether out of fear or not wanting to be a bother. Those who suffer in silence are easily forgotten but I pray that they can get through their troubles, seek the help that they need and be recognized by others.

Dear Lord, I pray for less bad news and more news to make me smile.

Lord, help me and the rest of the world to try and live by the example you set us through your son, Jesus Christ. Help me to be able to tell my friends about your presence and the relationship I have with you.

Lord, pray 4 those in the world who R going 2 bed hungry, unhappy or ill. Let them not lose faith in U.

I pray 4 more happiness in the world & if ppl were nicer the world would be so much safer.

20

For peace in our world

> **Prayer is not an exercise. It is the life of the saint.**
> *Oswald Chambers (1874-1917)*

Lord, give your children peace. Amen.

Dear Lord, help us 2 live together without war, in peace, and 2 love each other as U love us.

Lord, I feel your world isn't working. People from many countries and cultures are trying to prove their power and strength through war and terrorism. Please, Lord, bring peace into this world and forgive all those who have caused death and destruction by their actions. Let us join together as one world so that we can share what we have and help others. Amen.

Prayers for the wider world

Father, please give those in positions of power the knowledge and strength to resolve problems and conflicts of opinion by peaceful means. Please help people to strive for peace not war, and above all let there be understanding between different peoples and nationalities. Amen.

Dear Lord, please help us 2 stop fighting and teach us 2 think and talk things over peacefully, so that we can reach a compromise instead of using weapons.

Dear Lord, peace is still something quoted by politicians but rarely implemented. Please allow the most fragile area of the world, the Middle East, to achieve peace. Please help dictators around the world to turn to democracy, where individual people count as they do in your eyes. Help peace rule the world.

Grant us, Lord God, the vision of your kingdom, with forgiveness and new life and the stirring of your Spirit. So that we may share your vision, proclaim your love and change the world, in the name of Christ. Amen.

Dear God, may there be peace in our world and an end
2 war and fighting.

Lord, please help us to mend and remake this broken
world you gave us. Help our world leaders to make the
right decisions. This is the world that your son Jesus
died for, so it should be treasured and not destroyed by
evil gases and global war. Please help us save our planet.
Amen.

21

For our government and world leaders

> The real and lasting victories are those of peace, and not of war. *Ralph Waldo Emerson*

Dear Lord, please be with those in positions of authority, both in our country and around the world. Their decisions affect all our lives, so help them to choose the right things to do, so that your name may be honoured.

Lord, we pray for all world leaders.
Help them rule with a real sense of justice,
and a realization that power is to be used for the common good and not for their own selfish ends.
Amen.

Our Father, help us be more aware of the pressure involved in holding a position of power. It is the easiest thing in the world to look on and criticize. We do not see the full picture or the effort in areas that do not affect us. So we pray for all our leaders. Amen.

Lord God our Father, we ask you to bless our Queen and all the Royal Family. Please inspire the statesmen who meet in council to maintain peace, and to make the world safe from nuclear weapons. We ask that you guide and direct all who negotiate with foreign rulers to free prisoners and hostages. For Jesus' sake. Amen.

Dear Lord, we pray for our government and world leaders. Please give them wisdom to make the right decisions and determination to execute the right plans, and help them achieve a peaceful world for us all to live in. We ask this in the name of our Saviour Jesus Christ.

Dear Lord, please help our government and world leaders 2 decide what is best 4 the world of tomorrow. We pray they will make just and right decisions in UR name, Lord.

Our Father, we thank you for the world we live in, the food we eat and the people we know. We pray for peace between all nations, and that you will guide our leaders so that they can restore harmony into our world. Amen.

Lord, aid our political and spiritual leaders 2 endeavour 2 make the right decisions. Give them strength 2 understand the problems that UR children face all over the world. Help them avoid instability, warfare and starvation, and attempt 2 promote unity throughout the globe.

Lord, we pray for the world and all its problems. In the world you created there is suffering, violence, poverty and famine. There are endless world disasters and we could not begin to name them all. So we bring our concerns about the world to you and ask you to give your people strength in their faith to carry on. Instead of hatred and fear, grant us peace and hope. Amen.

Dear God, we pray for peace in our world. Not just the absence of war but good trusting relationships between all nations. Please show our national leaders other ways to end disputes rather than war. Help them realize that hospitals, schools and food are more important than

tanks and missiles. We really want peace. Please help
us to know what we can do to promote true peace in
our world.

22

For our Church and Christian leaders

> **If you judge people you have no time to love them.**
> *Mother Theresa*

Father in heaven, we pray 4 our leaders. Help them speak out with UR love and be strong in UR truth. Give them wisdom and courage.

Lord, each week you bring us together as a community in your love and fellowship to worship you and to draw us closer to your love. As a fellowship we seek to follow the path you have shown us and be obedient to your word. Help us, Lord, as we come each week to worship you, to get to know you better.

Lord, touch priest, ministers and pastors that they may be empowered by your love and not church rules!

Dear Lord, please bless all our religious leaders who follow in the footsteps of the Apostles by drawing people into your holy Church. The General Synod's decision to ordain women priests continues to cause division in your Church. No matter what our views are, Lord, we thank you for the reassurance given by your Holy Spirit that you will remain with us always, even in the deepest sorrow or confusion. Let the ministers of your Church continue to spread the good news to the world and fill them with your love and understanding so that they may continue to serve in your name. Amen.

Dear Lord, help the Church grow in number and in love and help those who go 2 church not 2 think it's boring or a waste of time.

Lord, I lift up to you our church leaders. Help them to lead as they should, honouring you and not stumbling blindly. Not with pride because they are in the spotlight. A church is a body, not a hierarchy built on status. So give them a vision of true service. Amen.

Dear Lord, please help our church and churches all over the world to grow and encourage others to seek you. Help us understand and accept your word. Give courage to those who are persecuted because of their beliefs and love for you. We ask that your love may rule *all* the earth and that we may live in peace and be ruled by love. We ask this in your name. Amen.

Dear Lord, we thank you for our church. We give thanks especially for all the people involved in the life of our church; for our vicar and wardens, for the choir and readers, for those who clean and arrange the flowers, for Sunday school teachers, youth leaders and sidespeople. We pray that by your grace, all the members of our church will continue to work together to further your kingdom. In Jesus' name. Amen.

Lord, church didn't go too well today. I thought a church was supposed 2 be one big family but ours is just a battle between young and old. Lord, help each of us 2 understand each other.

Lord, as we pray for the Church all over the world, help us remember that it is your love that joins us all together. We thank you for the friendly community the church brings and for all the people who work in the church. We ask you to bless them and all they do for you, so that your Spirit may guide us all in the right direction towards your love. In Jesus' name we pray. Amen.

Dear God, we pray 4 all those who R lonely. Please help us be kind and helpful 2 them. May they feel wanted and welcome in U R Church. Thank you, God.

Dear Father, bring all churches together so they may be united in your name. Help the congregation both young and old to be guided in worship by you. Often the young feel unwelcome in the services. Help the older members encourage the young, so that the Christian life may continue to grow and flourish. We ask this in Jesus' name. Amen.

23

For greater religious understanding

> Hate the sin and love the sinner. *Mahatma Gandhi*

At the time of 9/11 my brother and his family were working in Tunisia as development workers for a mission
agency. When they were back on leave in the summer of
2002 I asked him to come and lead a session reflecting on
our attitudes to Muslims in the West. At the end of the
session he asked the young people to write some prayers
about the situation and this is what they came up with.

Lord, please help Muslims, Christians, Jews, Hindus and
people of every faith so that we may create a better world.

Lord, help Muslims remember that U love them and
take care of their families and friends.

Lord, forgive us all.

God, please take over and sort this out.

Lord, please help us see that we need U, and that others need U 2 get through the horror of war and terrorism.

Lord, help us understand how people from other religions feel about violence.

Lord, please help the Muslim people when other countries take it out on them.

Lord, help us treat other people as we wish 2 be treated ourselves.

Dear Lord, the recent events in Palestine and Israel have had such a negative impact on our world, yet by so many they haven't been noticed. For some reason people

have tried to ignore these disgusting actions and inno-
cent people are being killed. Help us help them, that
they may begin to understand and love each other.

Dear Lord, we pray that the actions of a few will not
alter the view of an entire race of people and that they
will not be maltreated because of this. We also pray for
Muslims who live in Western cities – keep them safe.

Lord, help us understand and respect people from other
religions and not 2 be prejudiced towards them.

Father, help the families of all those who have suffered
as a result of war or terrorism. Show them your love
and help the leaders seek solutions other than violence
to solve the disagreements of the world.

Lord, I just pray that both the East and the West can
open their eyes and realize the wrong and the right they
R both doing.

Lord, help us create unity with the Muslim people, help us live in harmony as a united people with shared goals.

I really pray that with Jesus' help we as Christians may not judge others, especially those of other faiths.

Spirit of God, pervade and enrich all our world. Increase our capacity to love everyone, thus pouring out and increasing our adoration of you. Let your kingdom come!

Dear Lord, please help us understand other religions and their ways and not jump to conclusions about them. Please especially help Muslims and Christians. Help us understand each other and form a community where there isn't a war or pain or hate.

Lord, look after young Muslims in the West. Show them UR way and help them live their lives as U want.

24

For victims of racism

> We must pursue peaceful ends through peaceful means. *Martin Luther King*

Father, we pray for the victims of racism, we pray that you'll give them the strength to carry on their lives despite the discrimination. Lord, we also pray that the people who commit acts of discrimination will see sense and abandon their ignorance. Lord, in your name we pray. Amen.

Dear God, please help those people suffering from the emotional and physical grief and violence of racism. Please help them forgive the narrow-minded people fool-ish enough to make remarks about another person of a different race or religion. Amen.

Dear Lord, please help all those in the world who through no fault of their own R subject 2 discrimination, whether it be racial, social or any other kind. Give them the strength 2 rise above it, and let them know U love everyone and hold no one better than others.

Dear Lord, please help all victims of racism, and those who can't accept people of different cultures in their communities. We pray you will help and guide them to accept everyone, whatever their colour or creed. Amen.

Lord our Father, we're all your children, no matter what colour, race or nationality. May racism become a thing of the past, so that we can all live in harmony. We pray for victims of racism of any kind; and please help those who are racist to see the light of your love.

Dear God, help us understand that people are all the same, and that race and skin colour are irrelevant. Help us see through the outer person to look deep inside to discover our friend's true character.

Dear Lord, U made everyone as equals, so help us accept everyone as our friend, whether they're black or white, disabled or homeless. So Lord, teach us 2 love one another and 2 live together in peace and harmony.

Jesus loves the little children, all the children of the world, red and yellow, black and white, they're all precious in his sight. Jesus loves the little children of the world. Amen.

Heavenly Father, please help us live in racial harmony, not caring what the colour of a person's skin is but looking 2 the person inside, seeing only their good points and forgiving them for their bad.

Lord, help us not 2 see colour and creed, not 2 think black or white, race or religion. Let us live in harmony and peace. All R equal in your eyes, and surely they should be in ours too.

Dear Lord, please help those victims of racism who are bullied because of the colour of their skin, who are picked on because they have different traditions. Help us remember it doesn't matter what anyone looks like. You love us whatever colour we are. Help us be like you.

For when the environment is neglected and destroyed

> Don't judge each day by the harvest you reap, but by the seeds you plant. *Robert Louis Stevenson*

Dear God, thank U for making the world and all the beautiful things in it. Help the people who want 2 destroy our world realize that U love it and created it 4 us.

Lord, help us to look after this planet we live on. You created it and we know you would not want us to neglect or harm our surroundings in any way. Help us save endangered animals or plants, because we know you would hate to see them disappear. Help us look after our world. Amen.

Dear Lord, gradually our society is destroying this beautiful world you have created. Why do we do it

Lord? Is it that we're unable to see how lovely the world is? Surely not? Soon all the trees and fields will be gone. Towering buildings, flats, houses will be the only things the eye can see. Help us prevent this vastness of destruction and observe the beauty of this world and not take it for granted.

Lord, you gave us this world to live in, not to destroy and abuse. Help us live in harmony with our surroundings and think next time we drop litter or use harmful chemicals. The world is our home and we must not destroy it. Amen.

Lord, what R we doing? We're destroying UR world. We're killing UR creatures without reason for fur coats and just for fun. Help us see what we're doing and mend our ways.

Father, forgive us for damaging the world U gave us. For burning the trees and poisoning the oceans. Teach us how 2 care for our environment as U care for us.

Almighty God, please show people that the earth is for them and that they're destroying a gift to us from you, and that indirectly they're destroying themselves. Help all mankind realize that our world is a precious gift to be treated with care and respect.

Dear God, thank you for the world you created for us. Help us appreciate the living things around us, especially when we take things for granted. I pray you will help us protect our environment so that it's always there to remind us of you and what you've done for us. Amen.

Lord, we pray for the environment we live in, the quiet and peaceful countryside or the noisy busy town. Help us keep these places free of litter and stop people who neglect or destroy our environment.

Lord, is it right to destroy what you've created? Is it right to tear up the countryside to make way for high rise flats when there are derelict houses just waiting to be lived in? Every single animal and plant has a use in life, why do we ignore and neglect them, Lord? This world you've created has everything we need but slowly we're destroying it. Help us realize what we're doing before we get into deep trouble.

O Lord, you gave us so much beauty in the world we live in, yet we don't do our part and look after it. We neglect it, we even go so far as to destroy it. Help us, Lord, take care of all your creation, and forgive us for all the damage we've done. We pray this in the name of our Lord Jesus Christ. Amen.

PART SIX

Final thoughts

Final thoughts

I got a copy of this story from my dad, I couldn't find out where it came from or who wrote it, but it really gets under the skin of seeing the simplicity of prayer and how much we can learn from everyone's experiences.

My brother Kevin thinks God lives under the bed. At least that's what I heard him say one night. He was praying out loud in his dark bedroom, and I stopped outside his closed door to listen.

'Are you there God?' he said.

'Where are you? Oh, I see. Under the bed.'

I giggled softly and tiptoed off to my room.

Kevin's unique perspectives are often a source of amusement. But that night something else lingered long after the humour. I realized for the very first time the different world Kevin lives in. He was born thirty years ago, mentally disabled as a result of difficulties during labour. Apart from his size (he is 6' 2'') there are few ways in which he is an adult. He reasons and communicates with the capabilities of a seven year old, and he always will.

He will probably always believe God lives under his bed, that Santa Claus fills the space under our tree every Christmas, and that aeroplanes stay in the sky because angels carry them. I remember wondering if Kevin realizes he's different. Is he ever dissatisfied with his monotonous life? Up before dawn each day, off to work at a workshop for the disabled, home to walk our cocker spaniel, return to eat his favourite macaroni cheese for dinner, and later to bed. The only variation in the entire scheme is laundry, when he hovers excitedly over the washing machine like a mother with a newborn child. He does not seem dissatisfied. He lopes out to the bus every morning at 7.05, eager for a simple day of work. He wrings his hands excitedly while the water boils on the stove before dinner, and he stays up late twice a week to gather our dirty laundry for his next day laundry chores. And Saturdays, oh, the bliss of Saturdays! That's the day my dad takes Kevin to the airport to have a soft drink, watch the planes land, and speculate loudly on the destination of each passenger inside. 'That one's going to Chicago!' Kevin shouts as he claps his hands. His anticipation is so great he can hardly sleep on a Friday night.

So goes his world of daily rituals and weekend field trips. He doesn't know what it means to be discontent. His life's simple. He'll never know the entanglements of wealth or power, and does not care what brand of clothes he wears or what food he eats. His needs have always been met, and he never worries that one day they might not be. His hands are diligent. Kevin is never so happy than when he is working. When he unloads the dishwasher or vacuums the carpet, his heart is completely in it. He does not shrink from a job when it is begun, and does not leave until the job is finished.

But when his tasks are done, Kevin knows how to relax. He is not obsessed with his work or the work of others. His heart is pure. He still believes everyone tells the truth, promises must be kept, and when you are wrong you apologise instead of argue. Free from pride and unconcerned with appearance, Kevin is not afraid to cry, angry or sorry. He is always transparent, always sincere and he trusts God. Not confined by intellectual reasoning, when he comes to Christ, he comes as a child. Kevin seems to know God, to really be friends with him, in a way that is difficult for an 'educated' person to grasp. God seems like his closest companion. In my moments of doubts and frustrations with my Christianity I envy the security Kevin has in his simple faith. It is then I am most willing to admit that he has some divine knowledge that rises above any mortal questions. It is then I realize that perhaps he's not the one with the handicap, it's me. My obligations, my fears, my pride, my circumstances they all become disabilities when I do not trust them to God's care. Who knows if Kevin comprehends things I can ever learn? After all he has spent his whole life in that kind of innocence praying after dark and soaking up the goodness and love of God. And one day, when the mysteries of heaven are opened, and we are all amazed at how close God really is to our hearts, I'll realize that God heard the simple prayers of a boy who believed that God lived under his bed. Kevin won't be surprised at all.

A fantastic story getting truly to the heart of what prayer is, and how ALL can do it.

At the Cutting Edge

May your life in this world be a happy one,
May the sun be warm and may the skies be blue.
And may each storm that comes your way,
Clear the air for a brighter day,
May the Saints and Saviour watch over you.

Celtic Traditional Blessing